LOVE VOLUME

by

Tony Prewit

Love Volume

Published by Ridgeline Press
Silver City, New Mexico, U.S.A.
ISBN 978-0692882061

Editing, Tony Prewit and Patricia Prewit

Book Design, Lay-out Design

and Cover Artwork by

Tony Prewit, Ridgeline Press

Acknowledgements

I would like to thank my wife, Patricia Prewit, for the years of proofreading and assistance in sorting and editing all of my books thus far, and I thank her most of all for her being her and allowing me to continue to be the person she married. In addition, I would like to thank my wife for the proofreading and editing of this book. I am fortunate to be married to a woman whose skills expand into editing and proofreading. And most of all, she is my inspiration for this book.

Other Books by Tony Prewit

Six-book Series*: Journey in the Mind's Eye of a Poet:*
 Journal of Time
 Portals and Passages
 The Book of the Lost and Found or Chasing Rainbows
 Moods of War
 The Source
 Another Day

Spiritual Travelers . . . on our own without a map
The Observer

Table Of Contents

Introduction

Love Volume, Part One: Eyes For Only You is a collection of love poems written to my wife. I have also included other kinds of love poems in *Part Two: Many Sides Of Love.*

1.

There are so many writings, opinions and studies about *love* that it baffles me more rather than solves the mystery. The influence human love has on our lives as individuals and the human race as a whole is astounding to me. *Love Volume* is to be added to all the other writings, opinions and studies.

without love we become less human . . .
and without it we eventually lose our humanity . . .

i am not without love therefore i am human . . .
and a more complete human . . .

i know the need to be loved and
the need to love . . .

2.

Perhaps the love poems to my wife could be critiqued as repetitious, and are not necessarily in chronological order. They are a collection written over a forty-year period placed in the order that I thought fit the general flow of the book.

every flower in a field similar
> *yet unique and different from all the others . . .*

every rainbow giving the same colors
> *yet each new one is a new experience . . .*

every sunrise producing an array
> *of light in the sky new to us each time . . .*

likewise every love poem here expressing my love
> *using the same words and similar descriptions . . .*

every word, every line and verse placed
> *bringing fresh insight into each poem . . .*

3.

Free verse is my chosen style of writing poetry for this book. I did not adhere to rules of meter and line here. My expressions needed room and freedom to roam wherever the meanings of each poem led me. My free verse seeks sparse punctuations with a craft of style purposefully formed in a way to make punctuation unnoticed and unneeded.

i ran 'til i tired
i slept 'til i woke
i ate when i was hungry
and i am none the worse for it

all of this being part of me

—therefore free verse suits me well enough

Love Volume

Part One:

Eyes For Only You

Love Sonnet One

it was
fine as flour

and fresh
as a cold creek

it was the way
an eagle soars canyon walls

it was tight
as a cocoon waiting for spring

and how a
cat comes upon a mouse

it was a
fox covering its tracks

it was
love entering my life

it was
me seeing you for the first time

Embrace

the power of our embrace
broke the bond of loneliness
that has kept us until now

love is as powerful as any
force upon the earth
moving mountains
melting hearts

this day has come upon us
gentle as the softest touch of a hand
that brings us together
and secure as the strongest gate
opening to our heart

we fell headlong in love's grasp

Eyes For Only You

years have not
dimmed the light

age has not
erased the beauty

time has not
separated my desire

the more i see
the more i know

     —i have eyes for only you

sunrise
for the morning

sunset
for the evening

images of you
rest upon my soul

and fade not
with time

     —i have eyes for only you

Want Me

1.
a gust of wind
caused me
to fall

and i rose and
dusted my–
self off

then i tumbled
off a cliff
and crawled to
safety

i healed in
a few days
and continued
on

2.
i fear not the falling
and tumbling of life
but i do fear
being
separated
from
you

3.
want me
to want
you

 and be
 unafraid
 to let me
 know

Lost

i would be lost
in space
without
you

i am sure of it

Best Of Times

the first time
i saw you was
the best time
of my life

and everyday
i am with you
is also the best
time of my life

i guess one
could say

>*—i am living in*
>*the best of times*

Sunshine

i have heard it said
that we cannot live
without sunshine

    —you are my sunshine

Snowy Day

snow came last night
rumor is the rooster froze

smile young lovers
stay close and stay warm

frost came this morning like a
monastery descending upon earth

it is the frost that makes me lonely
the snow makes me stare

my love for you unforced
like snow falling unforced

missing you wanting you here
to watch the snow fall with me

i was surprised to wake to snow
and icicles forming without notice

we held each other the night before
you left with a promise to return

crystal flakes of white snow fell
last night while i slept

Love Volume

and it was an empty event
without you

my day is suddenly changed
i hear your footsteps on the porch

Bride And Groom

you my bride
and i your groom

we waltz down
the aisle of life
moving to the
rhythm
of the forever
       —i love you

Our Fairy Tale

in a land faraway
lived a beautiful young maiden
and a handsome young prince

they fell in love and
lived happily together
forever

—*our fairy tale come true*

Stride

taking the world in stride
     you and i

secure we sleep
     side by side 'til morning rise

living each day trusting
     love to be our guide

at evening-tide we rest
     our souls and wake fresh

the best years of our life
     are here now and yet to come

taking the world in stride
     you and i

Defend

i will defend you always
             right or wrong
does not matter

—*love defends its own*

When You Hurt

when you hurt
i hurt

when you have joy
i have joy

what you want from life
i want

  —willing to share all

Love Me

as i walk the quieter parts of the trail
i am swept up by the solitude
of the beauty of nature all around me
yet the deeper beauty of it penetrates more
when i can share it with you

the sounds of birds awakening at dawn
the cool breeze of the morning
ministering to my soul like nothing else
yet when you are at my side
the birds awakening and the breeze
of the morning all the more soothing

i could never find anyone on earth
as right for me as you inside and out
i am the most fortunate of men

—love me 'til the morning comes
and then love me more when
the evening falls and love me
all the times in between
'til there is no time left

You By My Side

you by my side
   my soul sings
songs of joy
   where only love
can make
   the melody
and the song
   come to life

you by my side

Counting Love

if i could count how many
times i have fallen
in love with you

it would be like counting
the raindrops that fill
the oceans

it would be like counting each grain
of soil that makes the
mountains

Answered Prayer

i prayed many times before i met you
that the person i would fall in love with
would fall in love with me as well

—*we are each other's
answered prayer*

Freesia Wildflower—Innocence

we fell in love with innocence

that brought us here today

like freesia wildflowers

our love blossoming

in the fields of

our heart

Living Plan

after many years our love

has grown strong

darkness and fear is undone

by the light of our bond

if a plan were made for us to be together

then we have proven it

or—if no plan at all exists for us to be together then

we have proven that love can find a match without a plan

whichever it may be our love remains

sound on solid ground

Lasting Love

lasting love
how do we know
unless we venture
with our heart

time well tell
our story
nothing gained
unless love is tried

if seeking
lasting love
ends in despair
can knowing
ourselves as
able to love
bring a peace
of its own
and draw out
souls like ours

reach out and
touch me
my love
we are real
and alive

Love Volume

with a lasting love
we try the world
resting in
each other's
arms

More Than

i love the dawn at sunrise
i love the dusk at sunset
i love the waves of an ocean
i love the wild in the forest

and i love you more
than them all

You Are

1.
you move
with a motion
that moves
me toward
you

though busy
you are
with your day
i peer
in

2.
the grass
on the hills
bends to
the breeze

the leaves
shimmer
on the
trees

the
shadows
of the day
move with
the sun

3.
and i am
moved
by you

as being
part of
the rhythm
of our
earth

Love Volume

What Matters

the love i have for you
like a sunrise
you are the first light

the beauty i see in you
like flowers in a meadow
you are the petals in bloom

the joy i have in being with you
like a breeze top of a hill
you are gentle with your touch

what matters—i love you and you love me

Stay With Me

the light in the sky is going down
the flame in my heart is glowing

stay with me

the look in your eyes
the poise of your silhouette against mine
is the love which stirs my soul

stay with me

i will never finish loving you
no one has taught me how
it came as naturally as the dawn
in the morning

stay with me

if we momentarily drift
may all the seasons of our love
be enough to catch us lest we fall
may we always court knowing
that we are the jewels of each other's life

stay with me

stay with me 'til the last moment of our breath
stay with me and forget not the first day
stay with me and i will wrap you in my arms
with the best i have to give

stay with me

you walk with a beauty all your own
formed by the trials and hopes that are in you
my eyes my heart and my soul take you in
wanting you always at my side
causes my love to grow
hesitate not

stay with me

That Which

that which i love in you most
is that which is the authentic you
from your birth

it makes all of you
more beautiful
and true

which causes me to
love all of you
the more

I Look For You Always

1.

as the morning light awakens the meadow
sweet perfume of wildflowers
rises up in the dawn

their petals showing their colors
as the sun peaks over
the distant hill

i reach out to touch you
and the day begins

2.

whether waking or busy about my day
in mind or heart
or spirit

i look for you always
wherever i am

There You Go

i found you

you found me

so there you go

as beautiful a movie about love

as there ever was

you and i

Memories Of You

1.

as the sun softly rests beyond the hills
the last of the light shows dew on the meadow

i reflect upon the beauty of it all
as my mind gently rests upon thoughts of you

your light forever alive in me
brings peace to my soul and life to my spirit

2.

first stars appear just beyond my reach but
i dare to dream that i can touch a star

you—my star and my dream
within my reach you are

we both reach until we touch
filled with love's awe

3.

from morning to eve
no matter where the journey leads

we walk it *en masse*

—we are one

Still Going Strong

i love it when your hand slowly moves
ever so gently across my chest
moving downward toward

your eyes stare into mine
there is no stopping
us now

the motion is set and what follows

our embrace so close that not a
hair could fit between

we take the motion of the moment
and make our own rhythm
absorbed in sweat

years pass and we are still going strong
which says something about
how love can keep
the flame

I Am Thankful For It All

1.
where would i be if i had not met you

i know of no other smile and no other person

as special as you to me

i think you and i wanted to be found by

each other

2.
how did our youth survive it in the midst of youth

i am not sure how but we did and

when we found each other we knew

and we are now celebrating the many years

i am thankful for it all

A Message From Love

we light
each other's
life

together
we are
strong
as rock

at night
we dream
safely
snug and secure
we sleep
sound
the night
thru

Everywhere

in my dreams you are there

    your life completes mine

you are all my years' worth

    you make me want for tomorrow

everywhere i wander in mind heart or soul

    you are always there

and together we are a home

Then And Now

i loved you then
and i love you now
and everyday in-between

Love Has A Way

love has a way
to shape us
into one
life

all elements of
our own
life
shared
to become
one

love has a way
to make our
lives
as one
life
worth
sharing

Would It Make It Better

if there was ever a day that could be stopped
would it make the day better

if there was ever a day that we could make happen
would it make the day better

most likely days will not stop nor happen at our beckon

so—i will count all our days as having worth
allowing our life to be molded by love

in whatever happens or not

We Are As We Are Made

i cannot imagine
who could fill my life more

if i could imagine such
it would still be you

we are as we are made
fitting neatly into
each other's
arms

Meadow Creek And You

i am three miles down meadow creek
just past the falls
the shadow of the canyon walls
cools the heat off my neck

my mind is full of the past week
but it slowly empties
to where the only memory that lingers
is that of you

      my return from meadow creek
      is much quicker
      the sun casts shadows
      and the colors melt into one another

      in rhythm with all the sounds
      of the forest and creek
      i make my way along the canyon
      seeing you in my mind's eye

      i smile because in a few hours
      i will be home again

      as i lie in bed and think of the afternoon hike
      i am also thinking of you and my solitary
      walk down meadow creek trail

          and gradually as i fade off into sleep
          i hear your heart beat next to mine

Living Love Poem

sharing all

and giving all

we are never alone

never at loss for why we love

with every word

line and verse

of our lives

Make My Day

make my day... kiss me

make my world go round ... kiss me

if you have too much to do ... kiss me

if you just want to ... kiss me

it will pay ... it always pays ... kiss me

There Is Nothing Else

we have been together longer than we have been apart

we have made more plans together than not

every step we make we make together

—*there is nothing else i desire on earth as much*

Simply Put

i love you
with every part
of me

simply put

my love
for you
transcends
all the complex
and all the
confusion
of life

There Is No Thought

there is no thought i would withhold
or dream i would not tell

i would not change any
thing that was
important
to you

i trust you
with
—and
in
every
way

Of Dreams

you are the one of my dreams

wrapped around each other as we are

no stopping our love now

All That I Enjoy

i enjoy the sunrise more when you
are there to share it with

a walk in the woods ministers
to me more with you at my side

my desire for an evening by the fire
is more secure with you close

      all that i enjoy
      i enjoy more with you

A Beauty All Your Own

you walk with a beauty all your own

    beauty from the inside out

one of nature's own beauty

    in bloom

When Two

we are of the earth
embracing the mystery
when two become one

one light
        one shadow
                one motion

Love Like This

1.
your love
lights
my life
with
your smile

your beauty
stirs
my soul
to follow
with my
eyes

your motion
is like
a motif
compelling
me
to you

2.
we
have in
each
other
what we
always
wanted
in a
companion

Love Volume

what
could
satisfy
me
more
than
life with
you

Grass In The Wind

a soft breeze
sweeps across
the tops of the
grass

you and i
are there
lying on
earth's bed

while the breeze
plays amidst
our embrace

> *grass in the wind*
> *bring your passion*
> *we are ready*
> *and willing*
> *to begin*

the sunset
and clouds
color the
sky

brushed
strokes of light
painted on
the horizon

you and i
are there
caught
in a perfect
moment of time

> *sunset colors in motion*
> *bring your desire*
> *we are ready*
> *and willing*
> *to begin*

Never Let Me Go

i am moved by the life in you
giving mine vision and rest

hold me and never let me go
i am yours

My Rainbow

you are my rainbow

you are my desire coming true

you give color to my life

nobody but you

Roses Given

the color of a rose petal in bloom

and the scent of its sweet essence

created to move hearts

a dozen roses i give to you

roses given in their beauty

like reflections of my own heart

—given

I Always Ask

a maiden i did seek to find
in her a beauty and perfection
and whose heart would be mine

one night our eyes did meet
one look is all it took for us
to know we were meant to be

and now every year this time
i always ask

will you be mine
        —now and always
                would be nice

Butterfly Song

i am as light as a butterfly

wings against the wind

i am flying to you

listen with your ear

i have a song for you

> *may our love be*
>
> > *simple and profound*
>
> *committed and free*
>
> > *awake and asleep*
>
> *safe and sound*

Enter The Dance

my spirit dances with yours
      in a rhythm we move together
our feet in sync upon the ground
      we move with the soils of eternity
we are our own melody and
      we are our own dance

      our love is joined

so while the days are ours
      we will embrace the time
making our spirits as one motion
      shadows by the firelight we are

      our love is joined

our spirits sing—
      fear not
            dance 'til dawn
                  time has no hold
                        where the spirit goes

enter the dance and
      give love a chance
            and the gods will join in
                  adding chorus to your own

All That I Want

all that i want is for us
to know our love is sure

and to open ourselves
unafraid to be ourselves

let our desire to be loved
make us desired to be loved

Forever High

i hold you
at the top of my life

—forever high
        and in love

I Would Rather

i would rather reach for you
than the stars

i would rather be possessed by your love
than any other

perhaps we can erase all boundaries where
love pursues

Always Know

may the valleys always be green
and from mountaintops beauty seen

may the skies always be blue
and may you always know i love you

though in simple rhyme
upon these words we find

> *—a poem's value is decided upon
> by the reader's heart and mind*

At Times

my thoughts wander through the maze
of our life together

i am caught in the whirlwind of time
years pass quicker with age

yet the memories of our time together
fill the gap as years speed by

       our journey
       our life
       our love
       our peace
              prevail over
              what time
              passes by
              and takes
              away

Bits Of Thought—In Love

     1.

in love—

count your blessings

be kind

find resolve for the unanswered

learn of your own heart

find your path and seek it daily

become who you are

unafraid

     2.
in love—

dive in

be you

merge

Love Bumps

our daily routine
bumps us
into each other

we lean into
the bumps
and linger

we brush our bodies
against each other
and slowly pass

we mark our territory
and then continue
our daily routine

these bumps
are the love notes
we pass to each other
every day

without love bumps
we would miss
each other
terribly

Brighter Days

my day is brighter
knowing i am loved by
someone as radiant as you

our spirits approve and
are more than ready
to play a part

Three Ways Of Love . . .

1.
how long does it take before a person knows they are in love . . .

the first time i saw you was enough time for me to know . . .

and everyday after that . . .

2.
if we would have never met

i would be spending all my time looking for you . . .

3.
what is it that makes me love you so . . .

it is you being you . . .

If I Could Reach

if i could reach into your soul

and leave you a gift

it would be a wildflower

that would never wilt

as a reminder

of us in

love

Most Important

whether the sun is rising over the eastern hills
or setting over the western plains
my love for you lingers beyond
nature's waking or
sleeping

whether i hold you in my heart or mind or arms
i am like a blade of grass holding on
to a raindrop

my love
holds
on

No Matter

no matter where you are
or how many years old

> *—time nor place*
> *separates us*

if i could say any three words
that mean most to you
it would be to say

> *—you're not fat*

followed by me wrapping
my arms around you

Fill Up Your Days

fill
up
your
life
with
what
gives
you
the
most
meaning
and
you
will
have
many
good
days

for me
a day
without
love is
a day
without
you

The Way You Smile

the way you smile at me

      the way you look at me

the way you reach out your hand for mine

      makes my day

now—what can i do to make yours

Your Embrace

flesh to flesh
     heart to heart
          mind to mind
               soul to soul

your embrace awakens
my every part

embrace me as you will
i am yours
to have

First Time I Saw You

the first time i saw you nothing else mattered
or was as important to me
as being near you

our eyes met and our souls met
that night we became
innocent lovers

from there we have followed the path
we started together that night

we never questioned and
never looked back

Be Mine, Draw Near

valentine
valentine
be mine

    draw near
    hold me close
    draw me a rose

valentine
valentine
look my way

    in me
    love
    you will find

valentine
valentine
wait no more

    i will wrap my
    arms around you
    a thousand times
    and a thousand more

valentine
valentine
sleep well
tonight

      knowing tomorrow
      and all tomorrows
      i will be there

Reflection

in a dream one night
i soared above the clouds high
where i could see the earth and myself on the earth

my eyes were opened enough
for me to see my life was not only about me

you were there in my dream

>   *come day*
>   *come night*
>   *come plans*
>   *come surprise*
>   *come dreams*
>
>   *no matter what comes*
>   *or does not*
>   *i am not alone*

morning came and i woke
there you were next to me

our day ready to begin

First Snow

first snow came

and cooled
the desert

and warmed
my heart

i am calmed
and i am sure

i am solidly
in love with you

first snow came

my senses were
awakened anew

It Is You

love has a hold on me
it is you
it is you

there is no place in my heart
like this love

and when i am heavy or burdened
i am lifted up

love has a hold on me
it is you
it is you

We Are A Pair You And Me

when we're blue
or happy
it is always—

> *me and you*
> *and you and me*

during hard times we work it through
and good times we sail onward free—

> *my kisses go to you*
> *and your kisses go to me*

all that we face we land on our feet
our love solid and sure—

> *more close than ever*
> *we endure*

Silhouette Of Beauty

silhouette of beauty
reach your hand for mine

hold me close
press your lips gently
against mine
pause there awhile

as the sun moves
across the sky
it beckons us to live now
while the day has light

and our spirits beckon us
to live now as if tomorrows
do not count

One Season

it took one short season to
fall in love with you
and once in love
i could not
get out

one short season for our love
to take hold

one short season to last us
a lifetime

Loving You

like the oaks that reign the forest
     and the hawks that soar the skies
and the rivers that rush through canyon walls

   the world is alive with you by my side

Like A Sunflower

like a sunflower in the field we began
our life together bathing in the sun
without care or worry

it was that time that gave us time
to learn how to love and
how to nurture

like the sunflowers in the field
bathing in the sun

—*we found love*

Home Is

home is how we make it
> some build with stones
> some with wood
> some have abundant lands
> some have gold and silver

but ours—be it more simple
cannot be penetrated or broken

ours is a life intertwined

All The Love Poems

if all the love poems were written
     and there were no more
it would not matter to me

     you are my love poem

if the last sun rose for the last time
     and light and warmth would not
come upon the earth again
     i would not care

     you are my light and warmth

if all the earth gave up life and breath
     and existed no more
i would still have life and breath

     together we are our life and breath

My Most

there is no other where my eyes search

    your touch embraces my soul

your smile brings life to my joy

    your trust is nourishment for my day

your love is my most treasured part

Of Stars And Love

add up the years and
count all the good times

      give me a star and i will
          trade it for you

What Is

what is a birthday but a day closer to eternity

      as if that would make us feel any better

but we do have each other and that does make birthdays

      an easier step towards an eternity

When The Sun

when the sun is tired of rising

        and the breeze forever ends

is when my love will take a pause

        to ask how will i love you then

without the sun's light and a cool breeze

        the answer is

        —my love for you has no end

Come Storm

come storm or not—

you are the shield
in my life

and years only add to
its strength

come storm or not—

we will remain safe
in each other's arms

we are the rock
in our lives

Our Journey

age our meter
life our journey

our paths are made
by the steps we take

together
every step sure

every horizon
clear and fair

Your Smile

your smile
      sweeps away
            my sad days

by all means
      keep smiling

Prayer To The Sun

sunset stand still awhile for me
make the moment last
i have found love

one day gone another beginning

we are all bound by the sun's constant

if i would dare pray to the sun it would be—

sunset stand still awhile for me
make the moment last
i have found love

and she has found me

Every Wish

every wish i have
every prayer i have
every day i live
every–
where
i go

i want you
with me

will you
        and always

My Soul Sees Yours

slender
with a poise

a look
that speaks

motion
that soothes

a touch
that warms

my soul sees
yours

i am touched
to my core

'Tis The Season

in a still moment
i take time
to pause
before the
seasons
pass me by
and the years fly

i want you
to know
you are
my beauty
my love
my life

'tis the season that reminds me
of when we met

'tis the season to be merry
and generous to all

my load is lighter with you
in my life

—must be we carry each other's burden
better than our own

Graceful Aging

—graceful aging hear my song

today is your birthday
so where is the meaning
in another year gone

i see in you graceful eyes
always looking out for others
and caring least for your own needs

time has taught you
not to close your shades rather
keep a light on for a lost soul to see

you found your spirit and
it bears upon you a grace that
allows age to move without notice

you are one of those who care
and i have learned from you
how to love better

—long live the graceful aging of our souls

Love To Love

brighten my day
tell me you love me

blue skies coming
morning sun rising

in rhythm to a new day
refreshed i rise

to greet whatever
ahead may lie

brighten my day
tell me you love me

confess
out loud say
i love you more
than life's charade

we are nothing to note
without someone
to love
and someone
to love
us

When

when horses linger in the pasture
and apple trees bloom with expectation

when the meadow sips the morning dew
and the sun moves gentle to lengthen the shadows

when lovers turn to each other
taking their cue from the earth

there is a time to say

    i love you

Come Early My Dawn

come early my dawn
beckon me by your side

so the chill in me
can absorb your warmth

horizon arise now
and awaken the hope in my soul

my eyes eagerly wait
so that i might see first light

as the morning rises
your colors reach toward the horizon

wake me from my dream
tell me i am real and i am here now

my love you are my dawn
reach out to me flesh to flesh

arouse in me my desire
awaken my spiritual eye

wherever i am
you are there also

come early my dawn
beckon me by your side

Writings On Flowers And Deserts And Us

1.
i saw a flower
bloom in the
desert
amidst
sandy hills
and rock

it was you

how is it you
can bloom
where
no water
is to be
found

2.
wildflowers
blossoming
in the desert

you have
found water

you have
found soil

you have
found light

3.
i fell in love
with you
when
i saw you
standing
alone
in a crowd
where
you did not
belong

beauty
can grow
amidst
strangers
like a
flower
in the
desert
with no
water
to be
found

—as i was saying
i saw
a flower
bloom
in the
desert
and
it was you

Love Volume

A Good And Wise Heart

born of good heart
is a beauty i see in you
and trust with all my being

time molds a good heart
making it wise and patient
making it with understanding
and a soul that is willing
to learn the how
and why

time
molding
a heart gentle
and strong

—yours is the good
and wise heart

My Spirit To Your Spirit

my spirit said to your spirit
    come
    be with me

your spirit said to my spirit
    i am willing

we both agreed
    and here we are

The Most Important Part Of That

the most
important
part
of my
life
is
us

and
how we
have
arranged
our lives
for us
makes
all the
difference

Once Upon

1.

once upon a solitary place
i imagined someone like you

once upon a lonely day
i needed someone like you

once upon a dream
i dreamed of someone like you

2.

*once upon a memory i must have
lived with you in another time*

*it must have happened to us before like this
i seem to remember something about it*

*falling in love somewhere else
in some other time*

Love Thought

the air i breathe
is fresh and new

love thoughts
coming through

Not A Day Lost

we've been together longer than
with anyone else

i can think of nothing else i desire
on earth as much

not a day lost in wanting it to have
been different

My Hand In Yours

my hand in yours
      we are complete

like a whisper we gently
      reach 'til we touch

the day will be good as we cross paths
      busy about our chores

occasionally brushing up next to each other
      like a breeze going by

we give ourselves rest at the end of each day
      evening wraps itself around us

my hand in yours
      we are complete

Must Be

watching tall grass in a meadow bend
     to an autumn wind

feeling the serenity of a snowy eve
     and the quietness of the white flakes

being caught by the movement of the day into dusk
     and the arrival of an early dawn

in sync with the calm rhythm of a steady rain
     bringing out the aroma from a field of wild flowers

these are some of the most beautiful scenes to me
     those i have seen and experienced

yet none compare to the beauty i see in you
     must be—the best beauty is wrought from love

Loving Husband (one)

to my loving husband . . .
from your most beautiful wife . . .

everyday is a good day
when i am with you . . .

we have created the joy
in our lives . . .

Loving Husband (two)

i cannot imagine a man
who could complete me more

if i could imagine it
he would still exist in you

you are my most cherished memories
and most favorite dreams

you belong to me

and i love you with all
that creation has given me
to love you with
—always

Of All

of all that i want
—is to be all that we want in love
— for us to open ourselves to each other
—for us to know love by and with each other
                              bearing the fruit thereof

I Sense A Presence

i journey not alone

i sense a presence
always with me

in wake or dream
i am never alone

i sense a presence
greater than us
which approves
of our love
and our
union
with
each other

Arms Open Wide

with arms open wide

stay with me until time calls for us
to move on to the next life

let us waste not time nor
lose the time we have

to enjoy what we have
here and now

with arms open wide

Together

together in spirit
and mind and heart

our souls are at rest

together our promise
runs deep within us

you and me becoming one

Wherever

wherever or whatever

it is a joy everlasting

living our lives together

as we do

Valentine My Valentine

valentine my valentine

whom do i love

on the mountaintop
my voice is heard

       it is you
       it is you
       it is you

valentine my valentine

the love i seek
has been
found

As Far As

as far as my love
for you is concerned

i see no end in sight

Looking Forward

quiet morning
restful evenings
lighted stars
against dark skies

wandering thoughts
coming home again
my life complete
with the love we have

—*looking forward*

Love Volume

The Only Flower For Me

you are my choice

in full bloom
with more color
than all the rest

you are the only flower for me

I Hold This Memory

i hold this memory in
      my heart
of a dream

      we danced all night
          by the light
      of the moon

         —like the song

The Life Now

we can never relive what has passed

i am ready to seek the joy
we can have now

how about you

If I Could Reach Inside My Soul (Lyrical)

how can i reach into my soul
and let you feel what it feels,
and show you what it knows

there's a fight going on
i need your hand
i need your smile
just hold me for a while

how can i reach into my soul
and take out the rage
and take out the despair

there's a fight going on
i need your hand
i need your smile
just hold me for a while

how can i reach into my soul
and fill it with rest and solitude
so peace could reign there

there's a fight going on
i need your hand
i need your smile
just hold me for a while

so 'til i find the strength to reach inside
will you hold me, will you love me
and soothe my fear

there's a fight going on
i need your hand
i need your smile
just hold me for a while

All It Takes

all it takes is a notice or a touch
and the memories of our intimacy
are turned on

we are as one breath and one motion
with every caress given
and received

the hours linger into the late afternoon
and gradually into the night
without notice

—and there is a stillness like no other

there are days we move about each other
in a routine like a single
movement

as we go about the day our silent thoughts of
our life together brings
me smiles of joy

—all it takes is a notice or a touch

Equal Gifts

rain for a parched field
sun to wipe away gray clouds
harvest for when the fruit is ripe

and love for our souls

—our gift to each other equal
with all the gifts of the earth

Love To Give

1.
you give without the asking
born with a gift the world needs
more of

i am most fortunate to have you
who has plenty of love
to give

2.
on a winter day the good snow
brings life to the spring
and we are cozy
by the fire

3.
many seasons and years
have come and gone

and we remain in love
and lovers still

Take My Hand

take my hand
never let me go

hold me tight
hold me gentle

place your body
next to mine

let us be the lovers
we know we can be

let not the burdens
we carry spoil the day

take my hand
never let me go

Love Will Find A Way

your heart
      like a light
shines for me
      i am yours

love will
      find a way
to make
      our worries
and cares
      dim and fade

Together

come what may
with you at my side
the world is brighter

forever may the tide
that moves us keep us
tightly bound

we move together
with the changes

our love is our light
trusting tomorrow
to guide the way

Give Me

give me a kiss
give me a hug

hold on to me
my love

passing time
draw us close

never forgetting
what the bond
of love brings
to willing souls
like ours

Another Year

another year older

and i am still

crazy over you

there is nothing

that comes close to

or compares

Our Friend

every year
   every step
we take
   proves that
age can add
   vision
to life

therefore
   i am sure
that age is
   a friend
to a love
   like ours

Each Day New

each day
new

every moment
unknown

rush not the
days

enjoy times
shared

let love
shine

Entry One

i usually wake early
around 4:00 a.m.
i don't think it means anything
spiritual or wise
it is just when i naturally wake
it is my own rhythm
and i accept it

many mornings i lie in bed
for a few minutes
and listen to my wife's
steady rhythmic breathing as she sleeps
she wakes later than i do
it is her rhythm and
we allow each other our own

i thought it was a good idea to mention
my early rising and my wife
so you would know
that i do rise early and
that it does our marriage good
when we allow each other
such personal time

Someone To Love

come my love
paint the sunrise
wake the light

come my love
we will cross over
'fore the river rises

come my love
sacred not the wanting
of lovers to hold back

come my love
arouse the earth
feel the gravity

> *brush the wind*
> *follow the embrace*
> *flow the sway*
>
> *we are but a moment*
> *waste it not 'stead*
> *live our life*
>
> *we breathe our air*
> *whisper our secrets*
> *for ourselves only*

Love Volume

come my love
chosen we have
a shared promise

come my love
live in the meadow
'side the creek with me

> *waste not time*
> *on lesser thoughts*
> *our truth is our making*
>
> *moments in time*
> *are all we have*
>
> *what do i want*
> *—not to live without*

come my love
horizons call us
look inward

> *i am someone to love*
> *and someone to love you*

Everything

my soul calmed
my spirit awakened
my mind alive
my heart softened
my flesh tamed

    when you entered my life
    everything in me changed

We Will

if the rain becomes a storm
who will shelter us

if the path becomes obscure
who will guide us

if loneliness comes to steal
who will guard us

if life does not live fair
who will defend us

                    we will

Part Two:

Other Sides Of Love

Win Or Lose

we love how we love
it is ours to be
as we choose it
or not

it is our love to use
and however we are
moved to love

win or lose
we are in the mix

Love—Forever Changing

love—forever changing us
   forever teaching us
      how to

   may our love lead us
   through all that life
      has

love—has many sides
   we have yet to explore
      them all

   and how to
      understand
   all that love has

How It Would Be

if you and i were birds
we would be redtail hawks
and i would search the skies for you
'til i found you

i would give you
the belly of a snake from
my beak and i would embrace you
and as we held each other
we would freefall
toward the
earth

and before
we touched land
we would part and
turn upward to the sky
and embrace
again

we would make
a nest together
you and i

Redtail Love

they embraced high above the earth
then descended together downward
'til the redtail's semen
made its course

then they separated just seconds before
descending upon the earth

and now the she redtail waited
for the coming birth of a replica
of themselves

redtail love is a mysterious love
as they meet in the sky and
embrace

they create an offspring as they hurl
downward to the earth

what in God's name would decide
to create birth like this

redtail hawk how did you know
that this would be your way
to procreate

Testimony

we are
never alone
with plenty of creation
around us
to give testimony
there is more
than us

we are
a creation that loves
despite the
mysteries of our
being

we give
testimony that there
is love
and love of all
kinds

The Marriage Orchard

i am in love today
yesterday and
tomorrow
two become one
in the marriage
orchard

Last Dance

the new year
rushed upon
our sweat

after dancing
we held on
to the
memory

we were as
one
both of us
as the joy
began to spill
its tears
'til dawn

this will be
our last dance
though god made
us for romance
there is a
dry gulf
between
us

our souls
stirred to the
rhythm
our spirits
danced
as the gate to
our sorrow
opened

we are drifting
by the minute
the last dance
will not last
longer than
the song
—'til then
we hold on

Jenny. . . *stolen before love had a chance*

      1.
gold as sun
summer days
and stars
like me being high

take innocence from the children
take wheat from the seed

the man said
reaping her wheat
in the sun
was so much fun
—so much fun

      2.
was it the harvest or the bird
who lay slain
in jenny's lap

i can see now
the sun will not last
the sun will not last

jenny run home fast
it is too early for morning
and too late to be alone

3.
it has been a while since
an unclothed moon hid behind
a willow tree

i see a girl weeping
please

her fear keeps the moonlight
'til the harvest

4.
she said
i dreamed i held a
dinosaur egg and
threw it high in the sky
like an astronaut going
to the moon
and it came crashing
to the ground

the man said
i will forget her now

5.
wind is flowing
over wheat fields
like waves
of the ocean

we are lost for a moment
come and lust

Iris

it has been a while since i heard your name
        and saw the purple you looked so good wearing
since then the road to tucson has been repaired twice

your being so much older understood the fool kid walking
        the tight rope was unaware
i was literally and figuratively blinded by the light
        of your attention

you left me one day after i returned from a desert walk
        you knew of no comforting explanation

we had no future taking midnight dips
        in the pool nude

you left on a quiet afternoon
        i fought off the human rain

thought it not good to believe in what could not be
        i could hardly walk to the market to feed myself

i stayed high on my grief for days after that
        my love is like a flower that blooms and
wilts and dries and blows away

—it all happens all too quickly to get a feel for it

The Dream Of A Hurting Lover

1.

i waited for you all day
believing you would come to me

i found out years later
that you waited for me to come to you

my love for you is like an invalid
waiting to be healed by your touch

the puzzle is that we both wait to see
who will rise first and knock at the other's door

2.

can i an invalid rise and go to my lover
though this be only a dream can dreams deliver

can i dare to trust the dream and go
knock at the door only to be rejected

is it of more value to rise and dare
or to wait and dare

my love has run and hid itself in the arms of my pride
for i cannot face the question

do i knock first or wait
whichever i choose it is the answer i long for

i sense that whoever rises first and knocks
carries the healing with them

and healing might not always have
the answer we want

Who We Are

good health
brings good life

      the life we make
      forms our soul

each day has
joys of their own

      we are better together
      than alone

we are of heart mind
and spirit

      searching for what makes us
      who we are

until we find love
rest is uneasy

once love is found life has a call
and a meaning

A New Adam And Eve

1.

a lone man in a small wooden ship
approaches a shoreline

aware of his loneliness
he screams his name to remind himself of himself

but the voice inside only repeats
a new name and a new history

i am adam . . . have died and returned
and i live in you

the voice haunts the man in the small wooden ship
as he sails to a shoreline within his sight

and sees on the beach a woman
whom he knows is named eve

eve knows the wooden ship leads her to her destiny
her loneliness lifts when the ship touches shore

2.

the voice inside her convinces her of who she is
she greets adam as he steps off the ship

her voice soothes his loneliness
softly and eagerly she speaks

Love Volume

i have waited for you a long time
now we will live without shame

you and i are alone on this land
rejoice because we are both here

we will multiply our own and give
earth a new start

I Am

i was an island
and i had sun
rain wind
and all kinds of
living creatures
and plants

i had everything i would need

then one day
i looked beyond
the horizon and
saw another
island

the unknown toppled my contentment

you—like me
an island
alone

the moment
i saw you
i knew
i needed you
in my life

even islands
need to share
their sun rain
wind and all
that they have

you were the unmaking
of the island i had created in myself

Eternal Youth Or Love

no eternal youth have we
yet something better we are given

    —a chance at love

    dare we risk
    to give all
    to the one
    who possesses
    our heart

    we need not
    chase rainbows
    of youth

    love is what
    our souls are
    searching

Love Volume

When The Fire Of Love Is Wrong

if we are the kindling
where is the match that will light the fire

if our hands were to touch the fire
would it be too late to stop

if a gust of wind suddenly caused us to touch the flame,
would the fire be fanned for sure

if so would we burn for hours 'til our desire was filled

how did it happen that it has become this way
for you and me

   may the match never be lit
   may the breeze not stir
   we do not love as love should love
   nor do we know how to manifest such a love

   all we do is start the fire as if love were a flame
   one moment is all it takes to be engulfed
   with a love that has no boundary or foundation
   can we not learn to make a better love that endures

   be persuaded my readers not to dream long
   so that it blinds you from reality

   if our dreams could remain dreams and still satisfy
   millions of souls would bow at our feet to learn how
   to dream such fantasies and be filled without
   need to live them out

Fates Of Choice

1.
i looked away
for only a moment
it seems
     and you were gone

you said it was
years coming
and you said
     it was too late

you said i had changed
and you said
     you had changed

i can hardly believe
i had this talk
with you in the
     front doorway

you closed the
door on me
the door to the house
     we had built

Love Volume

2.
love is not a doormat
it needs us to build
        and care
—then it has a chance to stand

if my love could begin again 'til death do us part
—would the knowledge and privilege thereof
cause my love to last and become
love again

3.
will i ever be able to call my love back
even with this newfound wisdom

i must walk this new place in life
and hope i have time to find love again

—we are fates of our own choice

Age Lost

where is your dwelling place
        —age asked beauty

inside
        —replied beauty

why would you dwell there when the
world seeks you outside
        —responded age

those who seek me from the inside want the
fruit of my life and those who seek me
from the outside only want
ornaments
        —replied beauty

            age retreated
                    and brooded
            over the loss of
                    its dominion
            over beauty

Timeless Beauty

two people in love
who age together
is a beauty that lasts

—*love is the beauty in age*

Ageless Wonder

ageless wonder

with smiles

and caring eyes

reaching out for

a hug and a kiss

time spent with

those you love

is the best

gift given

—just because

Meadows Know

my secret—you are in my thoughts most all the time

one day i told that secret to the flowers
in the meadow where i often walk
and the flowers were filled with joy knowing that
i think of you often in their meadow

> *flowers*
> *with a weightless aroma to fill our senses*
> *and a feast of colors to remind us*
>
> *take time to take it all in*
> *and let not love pass us by*

My Eyes Search For Yours

1.
my eyes search for yours
and a glimpse
is all it takes

with the right look
we give each other our loyalty
and our love

then my imagination takes over
and i create an image of you
beautiful inside and out

2.
i dreamed of you last night
and i watched you by firelight
you cast a shadow
in the movements of the flame

i watched you undress
your silhouette showed your beauty
you were quiet and contemplative
and at ease with yourself

you were taut
        well defined
confident
        at peace
and well cared for

i watched you 'til the light of the fire dimmed
i desired you as i always have
and before i woke i saw you watching me
then our eyes met and you smiled

      3.
as the dream fades i reach over to touch you

the memory of you this night
gives me peace while i slip
back into sleep

Late Summer

1.

it is late summer in the gila forest
riverbanks are
full of color

blues yellows whites and
reds are blooming
everywhere

wood lilies lavender thistles
gila rose and indian
paintbrush scatter
their scent

the gila river is running strong
and the breeze gives us
clues that autumn
is near

i watch you bend on one knee
and dip your hand in the river
you say it is cold
and i smile

my joy roars like the river rushing
through the rocks
here in the gila woods
by the river
with you

2.

i am full with life i am still

this moment will pass and i will
only have my memory of this day to
bring back the smile i have at this moment
                    —today is my birthday

Season's Reflection

it is not so much the time of year that is special to me
or how i celebrate the season

rather it is who i am with that makes it special

and learning how not to hold on to those who
do not return our friendship or our love

My Hand

my hand
reaches
for
yours

though
not always
visible

my hand
reaches
for
yours

Note For Young Lovers

embrace young lovers
move your arms and hands
and legs

press up against
one another

let this altar of love be built

though love can be elusive
as desert sand

though it shifts and it blows
with no guarantees
of solid ground

still love has a chance
to last forever

*fill our soul with a memory
of loving at least once without
thought of tomorrow*

The Chase

i chased
you

you
chased
me

until one
of us
caught
the
other

and
gave
in
to the
other's
desire

> *and*
> *now*
> *without*
> *the chase*
> *giving*
> *in is*
> *not*
> *the*
> *same*

Gentle In The Night

gentle in the night
my dreams of you
awaken a desire
that wrestles with
my conscience

i wake to find myself
exhausted knowing
my dreams search
for you every night

      —we are lovers there
      you and i

do i dare tell you
of my dreams
do i dare ask you
if i am your lover
in yours

is it better to dream
in perfection than
seek rejection
in this reality

      —we are lovers there
      you and i

so i will dream of the place
where you love me
and i love you

> *for what is the difference*
> *between a dream and*
> *reality*

> *if the bearer cares not from*
> *where his hopes come*
> *true*

Dare Me Not

cloudy day
energy high
cool breeze

    i dare me
    to look your way

i straighten up
stretch my
back
and gaze
at the spot
where you
stand

    i dare me
    not to stare too long

people crowd
the park

the festival
is alive

i must make my
move

my eyes are glued
to you

Love Volume

i dare me
to gaze without a blink

and patiently wait
for you to find my eyes fixed upon yours

a strange mix of defeat and victory

—*male egos complex in thought
and yet simple-minded in action*

Love Notes . . .

if you will love me forever
then i know i can make it
through eternity

or

if you will love me forever
it will make eternity
more bearable

or

if you will love me forever
eternity will be worth
the time it takes

My Love Has Gone To The Dogs

i was pretty
i was noticed
i married three times

i am sixty-nine
i am alone
and you ask me
why i have four dogs

they hear my soul cry
they notice me
and i am loved
so—

my love has gone to the dogs

In Times Not To Be Alone

in times not to be alone

in times of emergencies

in times to share joys and sorrows

in times just wanting someone there

>   *—we are friends that care*
>   *you for us*
>   *and us for you*

Fado One

this hour will last
me a lifetime
if we can
hold
each other
and share our
love
for one more
moment in
time

a cold wind presses
against our
cheeks
but i
only
think of yours
pressed
against
mine

there will be too
many love
poems
too many
lovers
who
aspire to
the same

but they could not
change this day

we must part
and hope
that fate can
bring us
back
here again

our fathers' love
of different
Gods
separates us

—as we embrace on this cold night
allow me one more minute before
your warm flesh and sweet breath
are stolen away

Three Poems

poem one

if You would take all that i have
it would not be enough to
satisfy the sin You say
i am guilty of . . .

the teaching is that we were born in sin
and all the sins from Adam 'til now
should weigh upon our soul . . .

i do not know if i would have known
the seriousness of the matter if
it wouldn't have been told . . .

now the dilemma of this information is great
is it so or is it not so and why would You
know so much about it and make the
writing so contentious . . .

maybe it is not You who claims but others who claim
and they say if we do not believe it so
then we are guilty of all these sins
we know nothing of
yet are guilty of . . .

—and this is supposed to be the greatest
love story of all

poem two

creator of all
what have i done
to be blamed for

i am as You have made

bear with me
show me grace

though You find fault

i am willing to learn
but i am not willing
to love You
unconditionally without
proof

> *—surely You are capable of showing*
> *the kind of proof that any one of us is willing*
> *to accept and needs—*

poem three

there was a boy who thought he could
no one told him no

he heard a speaker once through a window
dream big the speaker said

the boy did and came home with a bundle

soon the police came and took him away

they asked him why not be like the other
kids and learn to play

i'd rather dream big said the boy

and their reply to him was
then you will spend your life in prison

years passed and the boy did wake-up
from his dream and became a politician

though he never made a bundle again
he sure has spent a bundle

his journal filled with a love for himself
and himself only

without regard to anyone else's worth as having
any value near his own

Love Is Proven

if we are the only existence in our universe
that we can prove

and we are all that matters

    can we not engage each other
    and let the pursuit of love
    lift our souls above all
    the weights of life

        let us prove our love to ourselves
        by the value we place upon
        our known existence

            —who's to say how far the boundaries
            of love extend and the capacity love
            has to move us beyond our
            own boundaries

The Fog

see how the fog moves through the forest
it causes us to pause
and to notice the beauty of it all

we are stilled and we are moved
and better for it

see how the fog moves through the forest
we are overcome by the possibility of mystery
and to know what we do not know

we are excited with fright

see how the fog moves through the forest
will we ever get back if we enter
will it be safe

do i have what it takes

the fog as it moves though the forest
it is only for a while and it is lifted
but while it lasts. . . i seek its truth inside and out

see how the fog moves through the forest
it is as You desire
and moves us as You desire

You created it all
and You make us pause to notice
what we need to know
and so gracious to accept our attempt at humility

Short Life Of Melinda

a neighbor i never knew

melinda
born at full moon
above purple skies
born in the late evening
of midnight

—no one exactly knew when

       as her life only spanned
       a moment in time

call melinda home
she is of the lost in the universe
back and forth she is swept
by the wind of the stars

—every which way

       her birth gave her no time
       to make earth her home

she is a blue bird
flying into free thought
she is yellow
autumn leaves falling

she is a deer
drinking from a cold creek

—she is beauty that has no thought of a tomorrow

born of the full moon
swept by the universe
flying to nowhere
falling always
drinking without caution

melinda came into the world
and left before the day could
collect enough wisdom
to record her time

—she is eternity's child

> *born to live seconds on earth*
> *and born to live forever as a*
> *child of the universe*

Love Volume

www.ingramcontent.com/pod-product-compliance
Lightning Source LLC
Chambersburg PA
CBHW051958090426
42741CB00008B/1442